Writers Thesaurus Series

The Latest Collection of Mystery, Horror, Detective, Criminal, Suspense, Romantic & Three Elements/Items Writing Prompts

900 FICTION
CREATIVE WRITING PROMPTS

Written by

Muhammad Nabeel

Book Name: 900 FICTION CREATIVE WRITING PROMPTS

Author: Muhammad Nabeel

Edition: 1st

Series: Writers Thesaurus Series

Date: JAN 2017

Author page:

www.amazon.com/author/muhammadnabeel

CONTENT

Are you ready for writing challenge?

Let's Get Started

Chapter 1:

INTRODUCTION

Welcome to my new exciting & useful book **"900 FICTION CREATIVE WRITING PROMPTS"**. This is my first book of **WRITERS THESAURUS SERIES.**

This book is not only just for newbie writers, but also it would be prove a very excellent product for professional writers. It is very good idea to read creative writing prompts for getting started and boost your fiction creativity.

If you are newbie writer and thinking about writing your first novel, but you don't have any story idea, plot or starting line, here you will find 900 fresh and latest collection of fiction prompts for your start.

And if you are professional writer, and already had written many fiction books, but now you are stuck and not getting any ideas, then my book is exactly for you.

I created this book for in categorized way for your convenient. Just open your desired chapter and you are ready to start. I added almost all genre of fiction, but mostly, I focused on Mysterious, Suspense, Horror, Detective, Criminal, and Romantic genres. What would you find in this book?

Let's check this out:

Suspense, Mysterious, Horror, Detective Writing Prompts etc. (About 400 prompts)

Romantic Writing Prompts (More than 200)

Three Elements or Items Prompts (More than 200)

And much more.

I hope, you would like my book. If you have any question or suggestion, please let me know. So that, I can cover your desired topics in my upcoming books of Writers Thesaurus Series.

Muhammad Nabeel

Muhammadnabeel400@gmail.com

CHECK MY AUTHOR PAGE FOR MORE BOOKS

www.amazon.com/author/muhammadnabeel

Chapter 2:

MYSTERY, SUSPENSE & HORROR WRITING PROMPTS

Suspense prompt # 01:

Imagine, you are driving a car in the road. You are coming back at your home from your friend's party. Now, your car is passing through a long jungle. And it is getting dark. There are deep jungle on your both side and you are lonely driving on this road. Nobody is there.

Suddenly, your car stop. You try to start but failed. The car's water finished. You become worried and look around here and there. In the same time, you look a light in the jungle. You walk to the jungle toward the light. A few minutes later, you reach at the only house. And now you are surprising to see the house in the jungle.

You knock the door several times, but nobody come out. In the same time, you felt that the door is unlock. You open the door and walk inside. All lights are burning, but nobody is there. Suddenly, you look one side and you...... What happened next?

Suspense Prompt # 02:

Imagine, you are sitting and watching TV in your home. Suddenly, a telephone bell ring. You pick up the phone and there is some stranger on other side. The stranger said something to you and a fear creep over your face. Your legs start trembling with fear. You hand Shiver with terror. And you run quickly from there toward exterior door, and in next moment you are out of your home, standing in the street.

What did the stranger say on the telephone? Why did you become frightened? And what will happen next?

Suspense Prompt # 03:

Your fiction character opens the door on ringing the doorbell. There is a big strange-shaped box lying on the door, and nobody is there.

Suspense Prompt # 04:

Your character watching TV, suddenly, a fresh piece of flesh fell on the TV from above. You look at above...

Suspense Prompt # 05:

Your character is sleeping in his bedroom at night. Suddenly, he wake up because of some sound. He feel that someone is trying to break the floor of his bedroom.

Suspense Prompt # 06:

A story of the man, that become an invisible man by some chemical reaction. Then, he started to live his life in new style.

Suspense Prompt # 07:

Your character felt at night, that someone else is also in his room but he can't see; he is just feeling someone else presence in his room.

Suspense Prompt # 08:

Your character is driving a car, suddenly, someone come in front of his car and he brake the car and see there, but no one is there. It is third time when this strange thing happen.

Suspense Prompt # 09:

Your character take a house on rent in the other city. Your character knew that nobody could stayed in this home because of presence of some mysteries' entity.

Suspense Prompt # 10:

A ghost fell in love with her and don't let her for marrying to anybody.

Suspense Prompt # 11:

The story of the mysterious room in the hotel. Some unknown entity kill them, who stayed in this room.

Suspense Prompt # 12:

Your character decide to catch some ghost. So he cast a spells.

Suspense Prompt # 13:

Your character see a dream that some girl's ghost is living in the old cabinet of his store room and she need some kind of help. Your character don't believe on this dream but still he went to the cabinet at night and called her and then he shock...

Suspense Prompt # 14:

A bad evil that comes in your character's house.

Suspense Prompt # 15:

Your character cast a spell for getting a girl. And he success, but after that, he stuck in trouble.

Suspense Prompt # 16:

The grandfather's spirit of your character save himself every time, when some enemy try to harm him.

Suspense Prompt # 17:

Your character's child is sleeping under the tree located in his village. Suddenly, a ghost, that live on this tree, enter in the body of little child. Now child's life change he start to do strange things. Everybody shock and don't understand what's happening.

Suspense Prompt # 18:

Your character is reading a book. Suddenly, lights start blinking; door start to open & closed; his bed start jumping. Seeing that, your character faint.

Suspense Prompt # 19:

Your character with his team depart to investigate some hunted school.

Suspense Prompt # 20:

The darkness was spreading all around the cemetery. Suddenly, a dead body comes out from a grave.

Suspense Prompt # 21:

A young boy is going to his home at night speedily. He was late from his office. Nobody was at the street in this time. Suddenly, he saw a skull in his way. Meantime, a sound comes from skull. "Come with me"

Suspense Prompt # 22:

He had some mysterious powers. When first time, your character meet him…

Suspense Prompt # 23:

A mysterious and strange person start to live in yours character's neighborhood. The strange person never talk to anybody. He never comes out from his home. Your character's curiosity increase and he…

Suspense Prompt # 24:

He was very handsome and good looking man. But his eyes remained sad every time.

Suspense Prompt # 25:

Your character is going to somewhere in lonely road. Out of nowhere, a black can appeared in the car's dashboard.

Suspense Prompt # 26:

Your character is a tourist and he goes to some place and stay and enjoy there all day. Now it start getting dark. He sit on his car for go back. Suddenly, an old man come here and say to him "This is dangers area at night, some ghost live here so don't go right now; stay at my home and go back in the morning time."

Suspense Prompt # 27:

Your character is a writer and he went to a peaceful place for writing a new novel. And that lonely place is located in mountain hills. One day, he was sleeping at night in heavy rainy day, suddenly, someone knock the door.

Suspense Prompt # 28:

Your character is going to some village, but his car die in a lonely place and the village is 5 miles away from here. He start walking in foot and it start getting dark. Suddenly, he felt that someone is following him, he look back but no one is there. He start walking again and again hear some footstep behind him.

Suspense Prompt # 29:

Your character open the door and there is some mysterious old man. Seeing him, your character feel terror in his body. He start trembling.

Suspense Prompt # 30:

He was casting a spell in the cemetery. Suddenly, a can come here and he can't control himself and stand up. And that was his big mistake.

Suspense Prompt # 31:

She suspect that her husband daily goes somewhere at midnight. One day, she chase him. His husband was going to the cemetery.

Suspense Prompt # 32:

In the dining table, He was listening his son voice, but his son was not visible. By some mistake, his son become an invisible person.

Suspense Prompt # 33:

The story of newly married couple. His wife is actually a ghost and she drink his husband's blood daily at night.

Suspense Prompt # 34:

An old mysterious computer, whoever buy or take this computer, die immediately.

Suspense Prompt # 35:

She had an attractive eyes, and whoever saw her eyes, lost his senses. Then, your character fell in love her and after that, it started strange happenings.

Suspense Prompt # 36:

After die, her spirit was living in world. She wanted to fulfill her desire.

Suspense Prompt # 37:

Suddenly, his car became out of control. It seemed that some mysterious entity was controlling and driving the car. He was seeing all that but he was unable to do something. Then, car reached at a jungle.

Suspense Prompt # 38:

A dead body was lying & sleeping his bed room and he is being frightened to see this and he had a question in mind, "From where this dead body came here"

Suspense Prompt # 39:

In the first wedding night, her husband forbid to her to go to the upper room. One day, when she was lonely to her home, she find the upper's room key and she goes to the upper room and find something really strange.

Suspense Prompt # 40:

An evil that had been sleeping for many centuries, wake up and come to the city. Then, the evil started to kill to the young girls.

Suspense Prompt # 41:

A beggar comes to your character's home. Your character give him something to eat and after that, beggar became happy and give her a strange button and say to her that she should put this button in her purse for 40 days and then she would get a huge amount of money.

Suspense Prompt # 42:

Your character buy an old lamp and a ghost comes out from the lamp and cause many problems for your character.

Suspense Prompt # 43:

He shoot the old mysterious man, but the old man is still alive and had a mysterious smile on his face.

Suspense Prompt # 44:

Your character sees a criminal in the market and that criminal had been killed as a punishment.

Suspense Prompt # 45:

An incomplete building, that had been tried to construct many times by government, but they couldn't.

Suspense Prompt # 46:

A headless person walks daily on the road early in the morning. Many people see him and become frightened.

Suspense Prompt # 47:

One person that was present at the two different location in the same time.

Suspense Prompt # 48:

One cat was following him and he was running as if a death was following him. Who was that cat and why he was afraid with this cat?

Suspense Prompt # 49:

A skull was flying in the air in the bazar. Everybody was looking it with frightened eyes.

Suspense Prompt # 50:

It was the 25th bread that he started to eat in a hotel in lunch time. Now everybody looked amazed and afraid to see that.

Suspense Prompt # 51:

A far away house, it was said that some ghost were living there. Your character have desire to meet and see the ghost. So he decided to go there to meet the ghost.

Suspense Prompt # 52:

Your character wake up at night and become surprise to see that there is a light coming from his well. He walk towards his well to see.

Suspense Prompt # 53:

A lonely house far from the city... it was murdered to all family's members long time ago. And now, at the end of the every year, that house populate with their family members. Dead members eat & celebrate all the day.

Suspense Prompt # 54:

He was trying to find some blood group. For this purpose, he trapped the girls and asked the blood group. After that, he trapped the next girl. He had not succeeded to find his desire blood group. Finally, after 1 year, he found a girl that blood he need.

Suspense Prompt # 55:

He had such a mysterious eyes. In the restaurant, he fell a table with his eyes looking. Everybody was looking surprised to see that.

Suspense Prompt # 56:

When first time, he went to the shop for buy something, the shopkeeper gave him things but when next time, he went to that shop, the shopkeeper denied to give him things. So then, he needed to go some other shop to buy things. Why? He was an innocent person.

Suspense Prompt # 57:

A fear of spider that made her life miserable. One incident made a terror in his heart.

Suspense Prompt # 58:

A mysterious person, who could read and see the other person's mind.

Suspense Prompt # 59:

Suddenly, it started strange happenings with your character. Your character's things disappeared from place and then, the other time, things came back again.

Suspense Prompt # 60:

He was cutting the tree, suddenly the red blood came out from the tree.

Suspense Prompt # 61:

Your character is a taxi driver. He pick & drop the last passenger at evening. Suddenly, he see her feet that is opposite. She is an evil or ghost.

Suspense Prompt # 62:

A mysterious person who ordered to someone to do something and other could not resist. He ordered a person to kill someone and that person didn't want to kill but he could not resist and automatically, his hand grab the gun and shoot a person.

Suspense Prompt # 63:

Some enemies wanted to kill him but they did not know his mysterious power. The enemies took him a lonely place. Then what happened?

Suspense Prompt # 64:

Your character goes to the job interview and was selected for post. But when it is told him about salary that is $7000/month, a fear creep over his face and he reject the job.

Suspense Prompt # 65:

A monkey's paw move to your character's neck.

Suspense Prompt # 66:

Your character goes to some place, where it is forbid to go inside and written "warning! A danger place for human being". But your character goes inside.

Suspense Prompt # 67:

He told a lie, but after his lie became true.

Suspense Prompt # 68:

Someone fell him from 10th floor but after falling down, he was standing alive with smiley face.

Suspense Prompt # 69:

A person enter in a shop and want something, which was only available in past 500 years ago. He was the person of old century, and he had entered in new age.

Suspense Prompt # 70:

Your character get a stopwatch that can stop the time or age. Your character stop the age and stealing things and enjoy this time.

Suspense Prompt # 71:

A ghost try to take your character in his world.

Suspense Prompt # 72:

His sixth sense was really sharp. Whenever his enemy try to harm him, he comes to know one day ago because of his sixth sense.

Suspense Prompt # 73:

Your character open his eyes in midnight suddenly. He sees that an inhuman hand is coming inside from the outside window. And there are long hair on the hand.

Suspense Prompt # 74:

Your character hear a news on the TV about murder of himself. He shocked to listen this strange news.

Suspense Prompt # 75:

You are going to somewhere with your old friend, that meet you a few minutes ago after long time. You shocked when nobody could see your friend. That's mean only you can see your old friend and nobody else can see your friend. Why?

Suspense Prompt # 76:

You are sitting in your room and suddenly, temperature of your room increase like a oven. You become afraid.

Suspense Prompt # 77:

Suddenly, your character's dogs start barking to one side and there is no one there. It feels like that dogs are seeing something strange that human being cannot see.

Suspense Prompt # 78:

Your character is riding a horse in the jungle. Suddenly, horse stop and in spite of your trying, horse does not take a step. It feels like that horse is frightened to see something.

Suspense Prompt # 79:

Your character's brave dog feel great terror in second floor and never agree to go there.

Suspense Prompt # 80:

Your character take a home in other city on rent. And here he feel that his food & bread automatically finished in strange way. It feel something like that someone else eat the food. And he live alone in this house.

Suspense Prompt # 81:

A box of sugar slip and all sugar fell down. Your character look down and surprise. The sugar automatically start to disappear. It feel like that some invisible entity licking the sugar.

Suspense Prompt # 82:

A place where it is said that there are some paranormal activates. A paranormal TV show's team go there.

Suspense Prompt # 83:

In the night, a passenger's bus was passing through a lonely jungle. Suddenly, driver see a person in the middle of road. He stops the bus… Passengers were worrying that why driver is not starting bus again. Then, passengers found the driver died.

Suspense Prompt # 84:

A spirit start to live in a family in a face of a human being. Why?

Suspense Prompt # 85:

His father is scared because of bat and there is secret story behind the scene.

Suspense Prompt # 86:

In the midnight, a person is standing at your character's home. That person is looking very fearful.

Suspense Prompt # 87:

After shifting his place, they feel change in their little daughter. It feels like that the little girl plays and talks to some invisible entity.

Suspense Prompt # 88:

In the night, your character sees three persons wearing a white clothes in his backyard from the window.

Suspense Prompt # 89:

A woman was sitting inside a grave. Why?

Suspense Prompt # 90:

In few seconds, the pot of milk become empty. It feels like that some invisible entity is drinking the milk.

Suspense Prompt # 91:

Suddenly, a goat start talking to your character in human voice.

Suspense Prompt # 92:

He lose his memory. He does not remember past one month. But strange thing is that he remember before period of one month. He recall his memory; last time, he...

Suspense Prompt # 93:

A dream meaning teller tells your character that a big trouble is about to come and if he want to evade, then, he should do one thing. A dead body is buried in the house's backyard. Your character should dig the backyard for dead body and he should buried this dead body the cemetery.

Suspense Prompt # 94:

A museum, where the sculpture became alive at night.

Suspense Prompt # 95:

A mysterious person that whatever write and it becomes happened. So he made done his all work by writing. One day, he wrote something and...

Suspense Prompt # 96:

A person comes in your character's house from the future.

Suspense Prompt # 97:

In few seconds, a pound's clean water changed into red blood.

Suspense Prompt # 98:

In the morning time, he goes to bathroom and see himself in mirror. He scream when he sees some other's entity in the mirror.

Suspense Prompt # 99:

A doctor was researching on dead bodies to make them alive. One day he succeed but then, a dead body want to kill him.

Suspense Prompt # 100:

Your character is driving a car. Suddenly, a girl take a lift and then she kidnapped him on gun point. Then, she take your character in some building and force to your character to married with her in gun point. Why?

Suspense Prompt # 101:

Your character sees a dream and in dream, one old man says to your character to save his friend's life.

Suspense Prompt # 102:

Telephone that was broken, but it is ringing today. How?

Suspense Prompt # 103:

One spirit that was sending her written stories in a monthly magazine for publishing after her death too.

Suspense Prompt # 104:

He got a mysterious ring. By wearing the ring, he become an invisible man. So he started robbing.

Suspense Prompt # 105:

A necromancer catch a ghost for stealing and robbery.

Suspense Prompt # 106:

Your character is traveling in passengers' bus. In the jungle, it happened a fault in the bus and it stop. You and all passengers comes out. Suddenly, your character hear a voice from the jungle, someone was calling him.

Suspense Prompt # 107:

Your character riding a bike in the valleys. Suddenly, some invisible entity stop the bike & try to take him in a jungle.

Suspense Prompt # 108:

He goes to the doctor and feel an unknown fear with doctor.

Suspense Prompt # 109:

Your character buys a packet's of biscuit. When he opened the packets, there is some message for your character.

Suspense Prompt # 110:

He is going to somewhere in the rainy day. Suddenly, he feel that there is some invisible entity with him under the umbrella.

Suspense Prompt # 111:

Your character turn on the tap and there is blood coming from the tap.

Suspense Prompt # 112:

Your character feel that someone is following him, but there is nobody except a cat.

Suspense Prompt # 113:

Your character is driving a car. Suddenly, he looks a dead body in the mid of the road. He stop the car and get out, but now the dead body disappear.

Suspense Prompt # 114:

Your character has illness of forgetting the way in the rainy day. One day, he go to a farm house, which was famous about ghost.

Suspense Prompt # 115:

One spirit that comes daily in your character's roof at night.

Suspense Prompt # 116:

One cave, whoever goes there, never return back. Your character goes there too.

Suspense Prompt # 117:

He dream how to become a famous person.

Suspense Prompt # 118:

A college's boy, who was a sprit in reality.

Suspense Prompt # 119:

A college, where one student died every year.

Suspense Prompt # 120:

A Dracula, who disguise a human being.

Suspense Prompt # 121:

Your character see a human skull in the jungle.

Suspense Prompt # 122:

Suddenly, your character feel like that some invisible & heavy entity is sitting on his bicycle.

Suspense Prompt # 123:

He was running at midnight like that he had seen his death.

Suspense Prompt # 124:

A mysterious jungle, where money grows instead of leaves. All people run for money.

Suspense Prompt # 125:

A spirit of scientist, who was investing something after his death.

Suspense Prompt # 126:

A cemetery, where dead bodies become alive at night and go to the city.

Suspense Prompt # 127:

A person, who go wherever, a terror creep over the face of peoples. Why?

Suspense Prompt # 128:

His room's floor breaks a little and a human blood comes out from it.

Suspense Prompt # 129:

When scientist lost memory comes back by doctors, scientist was kidnapped by criminals.

Suspense Prompt # 130:

Your character see his stolen ring in his friend's hand.

Suspense Prompt # 131:

Your character got a bloody axe from the kitchen in the morning.

Suspense Prompt # 132:

A restaurant, where human blood is mixed in the cold drink.

Suspense Prompt # 133:

He finds a thing during travelling and that thing change his whole life.

Suspense Prompt # 134:

During travelling, a girl comes to you and catch your neck angrily.

Suspense Prompt # 135:

A few criminals comes in your character's home for stealing and then, they become frightened and run away with terror. Your character surprise to see that.

Suspense Prompt # 136:

A spirit comes & say to your character that she was murdered by your character's husband.

Suspense Prompt # 137:

A person was murdered by someone and that person's spirit take revenge and try to put him in a jail.

Suspense Prompt # 138:

At the midnight, his car start automatically without any driver and goes outside daily. How & why?

Suspense Prompt # 139:

A criminal was about to kill your character by pressing his neck, suddenly, it happens a strange thing and before that he kill your character, criminal felt that some invisible entity is catching his neck and then, criminal died.

Suspense Prompt # 140:

A criminal blasts a self-killing bomb and everyone died except himself.

Suspense Prompt # 141:

A woman daily make faint her husband. Why?

Suspense Prompt # 142:

At the midnight, it was a person wearing a white clothes on his door.

Suspense Prompt # 143:

He faint every time because of aero plane's noise.

Suspense Prompt # 144:

He sees a dead body of himself in the jungle. How it is possible?

Suspense Prompt # 145:

He got a mobile phone in a way and then, it reveal an amazing secret on him.

Suspense Prompt # 146:

A 100-years-snake who can disguise a human being.

Suspense Prompt # 147:

A woman, who take avenge of her husband's murder by black magic.

Suspense Prompt # 148:

A hut located in a jungle, it comes red rays from it and become a cause to faint peoples.

Suspense Prompt # 149:

Your character sees a shadow behind the curtain, but when he goes there, nobody is there.

Suspense Prompt # 150:

Your character hears a whisper in his ear, but nobody is there. Who can be that?

Suspense Prompt # 151:

A dog is trying to take your character to somewhere.

Suspense Prompt # 152:

A very important and famous person arrange a very thin & weak bodyguard for his safety.

Suspense Prompt # 153:

Neighborhood, who want to get out to his new neighbor from house. Why?

Suspense Prompt # 154:

He had been searching for his old friend for many years. Why?

Suspense Prompt # 155:

Alive painting, that shows past like a film. How it's possible?

Suspense Prompt # 156:

A jungle, who swallows to everyone, but some criminals are living there.

Suspense Prompt # 157:

Every car fell down from a mysterious road. But road was plain.

Suspense Prompt # 158:

He was trying to call to the spirit & dead bodies and then one day…

Suspense Prompt # 159:

There are skulls hanging on a mysterious tree.

Suspense Prompt # 160:

A person, who marry to a girl, and then goes to the abroad with her. He leaves her on airport and then, he disappear.

Suspense Prompt # 161:

A scientist who has many animals in his house. He does strange things.

Suspense Prompt # 162:

A person, who loves a girl, but after marriage, he hates her.

Suspense Prompt # 163:

A person, who hates to the children. Why?

Suspense Prompt # 164:

In front of their eyes, a glass automatically goes up and then down and break. What was that matter?

Suspense Prompt # 165:

A person had a gold ring. When he wear this, he disappeared.

Suspense Prompt # 166:

An empty & mysterious room in the building, where candles burn up automatically in the night and turn off in the morning.

Suspense Prompt # 167:

A jungle, from where screams comes in the city at midnight, but nobody has dare to see that. Your character goes there at night.

Suspense Prompt # 168:

He was opposite of his appearance.

Suspense Prompt # 169:

Your character has a truth about his friend. His friend take an eating thing for him and after eating this, your character would not be able to speak truth.

Suspense Prompt # 170:

A mysterious tree, whoever goes nearby it, tree catch and drink his blood.

Suspense Prompt # 171:

A cemetery, where one dead body become alive and goes to the city.

Suspense Prompt # 172:

Your character's husband goes to the jungle on every rainy day. Your character suspect and follow him. Then, she knows a strange thing about his husband.

Suspense Prompt # 173:

He slaps a stranger unconsciously.

Suspense Prompt # 174:

He saw a person of his resemblance.

Suspense Prompt # 175:

Their child react strange on every 31st date.

Suspense Prompt # 176:

He goes to someplace, and a sound comes out "Only ghost can comes here. Get out from here."

Suspense Prompt # 177:

She want to kill her husband's brother. Why?

Suspense Prompt # 178:

A school, where ghost's children study.

Suspense Prompt # 179:

In the midnight, he drink the water. He feel water's taste strange. He sees the water in the light of torch. He shocks. There is a red blood in the glass instead of water.

Suspense Prompt # 180:

After shifting in new house, he start to hear sound of laughing of somebody in his room. He became frighten.

Suspense Prompt # 181:

In the night, a white light comes out from the floor. He surprise to see that.

Suspense Prompt # 182:

Your character open the door. There is a dead body standing and saying to your character "I love you, I am here to take you in my world."

Suspense Prompt # 183:

Suddenly, television turn on automatically and a person appear & say something to your character in the screen.

Suspense Prompt # 184:

A mysterious post office, from where it is send mail to the dead bodies.

Suspense Prompt # 185:

A scientist, who steal the dead bodies from the cemetery.

Suspense Prompt # 186:

A sprit, who comes to see him on every 1st of month.

Suspense Prompt # 187:

Your character make a new friend, who is actually a vampire. And one day, vampire offers him to go to someplace.

Suspense Prompt # 188:

An old man, who hide his wealth under the room's floor. One day, some thieve comes to get wealth and strange happening occurs with the thieves.

Suspense Prompt # 189:

A 40 years old man is following a young girl.

Suspense Prompt # 190:

It is stormy evening. She became worried, and looking here & there, but no shelter is nearby her.

Suspense Prompt # 191:

He is very disappoint & worried. He thought to suicide. Suddenly, he saw a person, and he start dancing with joy.

Suspense Prompt # 192:

Music sound was so loud. Everyone is dancing with joy in his neighborhood. Suddenly, music stop and it comes out sounds of crying from neighborhood.

Suspense Prompt # 193:

It is snowy day. Everybody is on their house. A foreign traveler is standing alone on the street. He is trembling with cold.

Suspense Prompt # 194:

He was curious about that house, he want to know what strange thing in this house is. So he buy that house and then,

Suspense Prompt # 195:

She is hanging a picture on wall, then she saw thing on picture and she became afraid.

Suspense Prompt # 196:

A girl was running wearing a coffin-clothe.

Suspense Prompt # 197:

The storm spread all around her in lonely place.

Suspense Prompt # 198:

She hates him too much without any reason, and nobody knows why?

Suspense Prompt # 199:

Whenever some girl dead, he went to the cemetery at night. Why?

Suspense Prompt # 200:

Someone was in her room. But she didn't notice.

Suspense Prompt # 201:

This was a strange gift, which is never given to anybody before that.

Suspense Prompt # 202:

In this cold evening, she was going to her home fast. Suddenly, a voice came and she shocked.

Suspense Prompt # 203:

Suddenly, she heard a scream at midnight in her room. She became afraid.

Suspense Prompt # 204:

A wolf, who is a ghost, comes to the character' city.

Suspense Prompt # 205:

A ghost, who doesn't want your character's job. Why?

Suspense Prompt # 206:

He had been seeing same dream for one week. This dream frightened him.

Suspense Prompt # 207:

A mysterious room's office, where it is said that some ghost doesn't allow to come anybody.

Suspense Prompt # 208:

A guest house, a ghost doesn't allow anybody to stay night. But in the daytime, it would not happen.

Suspense Prompt # 209:

A mysterious person… Even poison doesn't affect him.

Suspense Prompt # 210:

Some invisible entity is breathing on her room. She was not aware about upcoming happening.

Chapter 3:

DETECTIVE & CRIMINAL WRITING PROMPTS

Detective Prompt # 01

In this assignment, I am giving you two characters and a thing. Can you write story around them? Here is the character & a thing:

(1) Teacher (2) A stranger (3) Weird gift

Detective Prompt # 02:

Those three CIA officers have been working on a project for two years. They have all record of some family. They are finding some point so that they could arrest a person. But in spite of hard working, they could not find even a single clue. All family records are clean.

Detective Prompt # 03:

A genius criminal call & say to your character that is a police officer. "I am going to blast a building in your city at evening, if you can save that building, come here, I challenge you."

Detective Prompt # 04:

Every Sunday, one person of their family members is murdered in a strange way. They were 7 brothers & two sisters in their family. Now three brother had murdered. Today, it is another Sunday and today it is alert very high security, but it happen another murder. Everybody has same question why and who is killing them. And most important question is how is murdered in spite of high security.

Detective Prompt # 05:

A little girl is playing with her ordinary doll in a park. Suddenly, a man comes there and snatch the doll and went away.

Detective Prompt # 06:

Suddenly, he wake up and see in his garden at night. There are two person that are digging his lawn.

Detective Prompt # 07:

One stranger threat him and say to take one small packet to somewhere.

Detective Prompt # 08:

He had been receiving one letter daily for one week with this written note "you would die at the end of this month." He became worried and contact to his detective friend.

Detective Prompt # 09:

A criminal steal some most important documents of the country and all forces are trying to their best to arrest him.

Detective Prompt # 10:

A scientist is traveling by air and aero plane crash. It seems that scientist have died but in fact, a criminal kidnap him for some dangerous purpose.

Detective Prompt # 11:

In your town, there has been stealing things for past 15 days. And police is unable to catch the thieves. So you & your friends decided to catch the thieves.

Detective Prompt # 12:

The story of beautiful lady, who is trapping a family's members in her love and after that she murder them.

Detective Prompt # 13:

She trapped to the richest person and then murdered them for getting wealth & property. The police knew that they could never prove that. Your character took that case.

Detective Prompt # 14:

He has a trained cat that steal gold & jewelries from the different house for him.

Detective Prompt # 15:

He made a strange plan for murder to his boss for becoming boss.

Detective Prompt # 16:

An astrologer that predicated time of the death of the persons truly and in next day, person died. Your character is a detective, he senses something wrong and he investigate the astrologer.

Detective Prompt # 17:

He was the cause of psychological mad of his two brother. He wanted to get property and wealth of his father. Your detective character investigate.

Detective Prompt # 18:

He was standing alive at front of him, whom he murdered long time ago.

Detective Prompt # 19:

A writer who write a book and all the story of murder became truth.

Detective Prompt # 20:

There are being illegal work in fisherman's village. Your character go there for investigation.

Detective Prompt # 21:

Criminal are passing through a place by truck. They are smuggling some drugs. When you character know that he reach there and catch the truck, but all truck is empty. There is no drugs inside.

Detective Prompt # 22:

Some stranger do phone call to your character and say that it is going to murder of some famous person tonight. Your character is a detective.

Detective Prompt # 23:

Some stranger do phone call to your character and say to your character to not go outside today because his life is in danger.

Detective Prompt # 24:

Your detective character is working on some case in outside the city. A criminal hit upon a trick and force your character to go back to his city.

Detective Prompt # 25:

It happen a stealing in your detective character's neighborhood, but it is not just stealing but also it is trapping to your character, so that your character go neighborhood. Why criminal want to call to your character to the neighborhood?

Detective Prompt # 26:

A very famous person is involve in illegal activities. Your detective character make a plan to trap & expose to famous personality.

Detective Prompt # 27:

It happens illusion to a person to be murder. He goes to the private detective.

Detective Prompt # 28:

Two person murdered in the same way. Both person got the marks of wolf's paw.

Detective Prompt # 29:

He was murdered by poison but the medical report could not prove that.

Detective Prompt # 30:

After ten years, you detective character meet his friend by chance. You friend offers to your character for some illegal job or work and friend don't know about your character that he is detective.

Detective Prompt # 31:

Three person wanted to get some doll. Why?

Detective Prompt # 32:

He want to become an honest busman but he needs money. So he tried to get money in wrong way for his honest business.

Detective Prompt # 33:

Your character buys a new car. And in next day, a police officer says to your character that this car used in an illegal activities yesterday.

Detective Prompt # 34:

Some criminals were using the criminal methods that were written by famous fiction detective writer.

Detective Prompt # 35:

An employ of a detective person, who had two faces: one innocent employ and the other clever criminal.

Detective Prompt # 36:

A car is running without any driver. Suddenly, the empty car follow a person and try to kill him. Finally, the car crush him.

Detective Prompt # 37:

He has two faces, writer & a boss of criminal group. He give important messages and orders to his group members by writing a book. Your character investigate.

Detective Prompt # 38:

It was the travel of 40 days of motor boat. It was 50 passengers in this big motor boat. Suddenly, a person was murdered in mysterious way and then, the other day it happened another murder. Your detective character is also traveling, so he investigate.

Detective Prompt # 39:

Your character find a dead body in the backyard at morning.

Detective Prompt # 40:

A big treasure comes out in your character's house after digging the yard.

Detective Prompt # 40:

When your detective character reached there for catching the criminal, the criminal is already murdered.

Detective Prompt # 41:

His wife is kidnapped on first night of wedding.

Detective Prompt # 42:

Murder's location prove that criminal has only one leg.

Detective Prompt # 43:

Your detective character catch the criminal because of just a single piece of cigar.

Detective Prompt # 44:

Your character finds a dead body on his door.

Detective Prompt # 45:

Your character finds a dead body on his refrigerator.

Detective Prompt # 46:

He was running a garment's business but behind the scene, he is included in illegal activities.

Detective Prompt # 47:

A story of innocent man whose crime was, to not be a criminal.

Detective Prompt # 48:

A person was standing in front of building and watching his watch. As soon as it strike 12'o clock, he press the button.

Detective Prompt # 49:

One criminal was traveling in your character's car, and you don't know about that.

Detective Prompt # 50:

Your character receive a gift and in this gift, there is a piece of human hand.

Detective Prompt # 51:

Your character receive an email, "You are murdered today at 4:00 pm."

Detective Prompt # 52:

Your detective character is chasing a criminal. Criminal entered In a small both and then disappear, when your character enter there.

Detective Prompt # 53:

An eyewitness is saying that your character murdered to a man. But in fact, it is not true.

Detective Prompt # 54:

Your character buy a new trunk, when he come back at his home and open it, there is a dead body in the trunk.

Detective Prompt # 55:

Her husband is murdered in a mysterious way. She is suspecting to husband's brother.

Detective Prompt # 56:

One balled man is murdered. And a comb comes out from his pocket.

Detective Prompt # 57:

One person who steal the things unconsciously.

Detective Prompt # 58:

A strange case comes to your detective character. She says to him that a dead body want to kill her. Your character surprised to hear this.

Detective Prompt # 59:

A criminal who had dead few years ago, but in fact, he was alive. So this thing goes in his favor, and he started illegal work again.

Detective Prompt # 60:

He was suspecting about her wife, that her wife is going to kill him. So he contact to a detective, but after five years passing, he is still alive. Now he become satisfy, and then, few day later, he was murdered in a mysterious way.

Detective Prompt # 61:

A taxi drive drops his last passenger in a destination. When he come back, he got a gift in his taxi and it was written "taxi driver! Instantly pick & drop this gift in that location."

Detective Prompt # 62:

He was saying to a waiter "I would give you $10000, if you threw the dead body in the ocean or jungle."

Detective Prompt # 63:

A 40 years man had married in 10 times, and every time, his wife died. Why?

Detective Prompt # 64:

Daughter of prime minster are kidnapped and kidnapper are demanding that prime minister should resigned.

Detective Prompt # 65:

A person is murdered and detective find this written piece of paper there "I am going to suicide."

Detective Prompt # 66:

There are two genus students who can first position in the college. But one student is murdered.

Detective Prompt # 67:

She is very beautiful murderer. Many detective tried to catch her but in the last movement, they failed. How & why?

Detective Prompt # 68:

He became a mental case after love marriage. Why?

Detective Prompt # 69:

Your character goes to a restaurant with his friend, and take a tea. With first sip, his friend faint.

Detective Prompt # 70:

It happens a stealing in the neighborhood and all the things is found in your character's home. And In fact he is not a thief.

Detective Prompt # 71:

Some criminal rumor about a building and say, there are some ghost who lives in this building. Then, those criminal start living there.

Detective Prompt # 72:

A famous person is murdered. Your detective finds a message written by blood in the location, where the person is murdered.

Detective Prompt # 73:

A criminal disappear from the jail in the night.

Detective Prompt # 74:

A criminal, who disguise a police officer & enter in your character's house.

Detective Prompt # 75:

A person, who recognizes the criminal, but by a trick, his memory was lost.

Detective Prompt # 76:

Some criminals kidnap a scientist. When your detective investigate, a secret was revealed.

Detective Prompt # 77:

Your character show her gold jewelry to her neighborhood and the next day, it is stolen.

Detective Prompt # 78:

Your character's pistol is used in some illegal activities and you character doesn't know that.

Detective Prompt # 79:

A boss of criminal group is kidnapped by someone.

Detective Prompt # 80:

Some criminals take away an ordinary ring from your character.

Detective Prompt # 81:

Some criminals steal just an ordinary watch from your character's house.

Detective Prompt # 82:

He finds his stolen bike in front of some house.

Detective Prompt # 83:

He goes to see her girlfriend. But he finds her dead body in her apartment. She was murdered by someone.

Detective Prompt # 84:

An eye witness person disguise a ghost and frighten to the murderer.

Detective Prompt # 85:

During travelling, he lost his wallet, he suspect to a passenger.

Detective Prompt # 86:

He was an honest officer, but he is trapped by a clever man. And he do an illegal work.

Detective Prompt # 87:

An enemy injects an injection to your character's dog and dog got mad and attract to your character.

Detective Prompt # 88:

She murder her husband and flee away with his boyfriend.

Detective Prompt # 89:

Your detective character's loyal assistant attacks to him. Why?

Detective Prompt # 90:

Some criminals kidnap your character's assistant.

Detective Prompt # 91:

Your character return his home and see all door opened by some thieves but nothing was stolen.

Detective Prompt # 92:

Your character pick & drop a child to his home, who forget his home's way but child tells to his parents that he was kidnaped by your character.

Detective Prompt # 93:

A criminal disguise a needy person and start to live in your character's home.

Detective Prompt # 94:

A woman got success to find her husband's murderer.

Detective Prompt # 95:

Your character's second husband is about to kill her son in a strange way, but your character comes to know.

Detective Prompt # 96:

A friends invite to your character on dinner and want to kill him by poison food, but your character suspects.

Detective Prompt # 97:

Someone has been following to your character for two days, but your character is not knows about that.

Detective Prompt # 98:

Your character have many dogs. One day, his one dog got mad, the other day another dog got mad. Why it's happing?

Detective Prompt # 99:

A very important file of government is stolen.

Detective Prompt # 100:

He got up and finds many cockroaches around him. He becomes frighten. Your detective character knows that someone tried to kill that guy.

Detective Prompt # 101:

Someone has been attacking on your character for some days.

Detective Prompt # 102:

A park far away from city, where peoples go and lost his memory.

Detective Prompt # 103:

Your detective character's assistant is murdered.

Detective Prompt # 104:

A mysterious murder of security guard, someone made her neck in opposite side.

Detective Prompt # 105:

An innocent person who become notorious as a criminal.

Detective Prompt # 106:

A person, who start to kill every beautiful girl after his failure in love.

Detective Prompt # 107:

Your character's money disappear daily. Why?

Detective Prompt # 108:

In a friend's party, your friend's money is stolen and then, the money is found in your character's pocket.

Detective Prompt # 109:

A bear is stealing in the city. And nobody knows that.

Detective Prompt # 110:

Your character knows a criminal, whom police is trying to catch.

Detective Prompt # 111:

Your character is an eye witness of a murder but he doesn't tell to the police.

Detective Prompt # 112:

A criminal who force to the people for suicide.

Detective Prompt # 113:

An important file of government, that is stolen, your character got this by chance. And he don't know about its importance.

Detective Prompt # 114:

Your character got secret from a criminal groups by disguising a criminal.

Detective Prompt # 115:

Your character got a dead body of person, who had disappeared.

Detective Prompt # 116:

Your character sees a person, who is throwing a dead body in ocean.

Detective Prompt # 117:

A signer, who is a criminal in reality.

Detective Prompt # 118:

Your character catch a criminal by a piece of cigar.

Detective Prompt # 119:

A shopkeeper who is selling human blood. Why?

Detective Prompt # 120:

On gun point, his car is robbed and after one hours, he finds his car in front of his house.

Detective Prompt # 121:

Three women are claiming about a child that those are mother of her.

Detective Prompt # 122:

While getting the water from well, a dead body comes out from the well.

Detective Prompt # 123:

An orphan man was boss of criminal group. Nobody can think that.

Detective Prompt # 124:

A famous detective is kidnapped.

Detective Prompt # 125:

He is a criminal, but in reality, he is working for his country.

Detective Prompt # 126:

Suddenly, three person start claiming to be owner of your character's property.

Detective Prompt # 127:

She suspect about her husband to be a criminal. She contact with a detective.

Detective Prompt # 128:

He is a murderer of three guys. And he is pretending to be a mental.

Detective Prompt # 129:

He is an honest police officer but after an accident, he became a criminal.

Detective Prompt # 130:

A headquarters of criminals is under the sea. Your character goes under the sea.

Detective Prompt # 131:

He doesn't know about his two faces. In night, he is clever criminal but in day, he was a genius detective.

Detective Prompt # 132:

Your detective character comes to know that a big criminal is coming in his country.

Detective Prompt # 133:

In his first night of wedding, he try to kill his wife. Why?

Detective Prompt # 134:

Many peoples want to buy a specific idol and idol's price increase and reach at 20 billion dollars, but in spite of that, many peoples want to buy it. Why?

Detective Prompt # 135:

In the mental hospital, a person, who is not mental in reality, is living for a purpose.

Detective Prompt # 136:

A criminal comes to your character's house for save his life.

Detective Prompt # 137:

By Mistake, your character is kidnapped because of resemblance of a rich man.

Detective Prompt # 138:

Your character comes to know that a famous person would be killed tonight. Your character contact to the police officer, but they can't listen to him and at night, famous person is killed by someone.

Detective Prompt # 139:

A police officer fell in love with a criminal girl.

Detective Prompt # 140:

A stranger comes & give a diamond of necklace to your character.

Detective Prompt # 141:

A person comes and say to waiter "if someone have chance to get 2500 dollar in just 10 minutes work, what should he do?"

Detective Prompt # 142:

A stranger offered a huge amount of money to a poor man for illegal work.

Detective Prompt # 143:

At midnight, a beautiful girl comes to his door, and want to stay for one night. He allows her to stay for one night. In the morning, she murder him. Why?

Detective Prompt # 144:

A beautiful girl used to trapping to the boys and after that, she killed him. Why?

Detective Prompt # 145:

He had been planning to kill his business partner and today, he got a chance to kill him.

Detective Prompt # 146:

An innocent man is standing in the court. Your genius character save him.

Detective Prompt # 147:

On charismas event, she invited to murderer of his father. She want revenge.

Detective Prompt # 148:

Her grandson was enemy of her and they made her orphan.

Detective Prompt # 149:

A clever sister, who murder his sister's husband. Finally, secret reveal.

Detective Prompt # 150:

He gives a gift to a person. And in this gift, there is a bomb.

Detective Prompt # 151:

What was in the plate, that he became ill after eating that?

Detective Prompt # 152:

She tired, while saving her child from enemies.

Detective Prompt # 153:

A person comes to your detective character and tells about a murderer. Your character six sense is saying that he is lying.

Detective Prompt # 154:

A person is running holding a dead body in his hand. Your detective character sees him by chance.

Detective Prompt # 155:

A 12 years old boy comes to your detective character's home and say, I am going to tell about a criminal.

Detective Prompt # 156:

A 10 years old girl comes & say to your detective character that she is here to protect him.

Detective Prompt # 157:

Your character sense some shadow on the window.

Detective Prompt # 158:

Someone is sitting your character's room for returning an important file that your character had lost two days ago.

Detective Prompt # 159:

Your character start his car, suddenly he saw a knife with red blood on car's dashboard.

Detective Prompt # 160:

Your detective character is following a criminal, and then, a girl come in front of car, so he has to stop his car. And then, criminal flee away.

Chapter 6:

ROMANTIC & SOCIAL WRITING PROMPTS

Romantic Prompt # 01:

A newly married person fell in love with his wife's sister, when he saw her first time.

Romantic Prompt # 02:

Your character suspect that his husband is having an affair, so she start to keep an eye on his husband, then she finds something that she was not expecting.

Romantic Prompt # 03:

Your character fell in love with one girl, who insulted him in a party.

Romantic Prompt # 04:

In a party, your character is sitting with his beloved husband. Suddenly, a person comes and says to your character that he and she both loved to each other a long time ago. You character become surprise to hear this. Because she doesn't know him.

Romantic Prompt # 05:

Your character goes to the central library and fell in love with librarian.

Romantic Prompt # 06:

Your character is a big fan of a young writer. He always read his fiction romantic book. And after few times, your character fell in love with the writer and decide to take action.

Romantic Prompt # 07:

Your character see a beautiful girl in his dream at night, and then, he fell in love with this girl. One day, he saw that girl in a restaurant.

Romantic Prompt # 08:

A girl start to like his boss and boss is already married.

Romantic Prompt # 09:

After five years of their friendship, guy angry with the girl and decide to left her.

Romantic Prompt # 10:

Your character is big cheater, who have deceived to many girls. One day, he fell in love with a cheater girl, who have looted the wealth of many men.

Romantic Prompt # 11:

Your character cast a spells for getting true love.

Romantic Prompt # 12:

Your character fell in love with a girl's painting created by an artist.

Romantic Prompt # 13:

Your character's husband unnecessarily suspect her. After passing some times, your character became so annoy and then, she start an affair for punishing her husband.

Romantic Prompt # 14:

A person had been watching to this girl continually for past four days.

Romantic Prompt # 15:

Your character lost his passport in other country.

Romantic Prompt # 16:

One day your character read his husband's dairy by chance and he get a strange secret about his husband.

Romantic Prompt # 17:

She married with a 60-years-old person. She was afraid and she was praying that old person is not be already married. She can tolerate everything except husband's wife.

Romantic Prompt # 18:

She fell in love with his step son.

Romantic Prompt # 19:

Some robbers loot your character's car and other things in abroad on lonely place where you don't know how to come back at your home without any vehicles.

Romantic Prompt # 20:

Your character's husband is trying to find some reason to divorce her and she is avoiding.

Romantic Prompt # 21:

Your character's husband got promotion, and many girls start liking him and want to marry him.

Romantic Prompt # 22:

One day, your character's husband got another married.

Romantic Prompt # 23:

One rich girl, who would die in one year because of cancer, offer a poor boy for marrying with her.

Romantic Prompt # 24:

One day, your character knows that her poor husband has too much money in realty, and he is just pretending as a poor man.

Romantic Prompt # 25:

He suspects that his wife is giving things one by one to someone.

Romantic Prompt # 26:

The old man suspect that his wife would leave him one day. But that is not true in fact.

Romantic Prompt # 27:

Your character's third wife leave him. Why it happens every time with him? Why wives left him?

Romantic Prompt # 28:

He wanted to marry a girl who had A-negative blood group. He had been finding such a girl for long times.

Romantic Prompt # 29:

A girl cheat your character, and then, he become an abnormal person, and he started cheating to every girl.

Romantic Prompt # 30:

He fell in love with a girl, when he saw her in a shopping mall.

Romantic Prompt # 31:

She hate too much with name of 'Robert'. Whenever she saw a person whose name is 'Robert', she react strangely.

Romantic Prompt # 32:

She fell in love with a boy, who is enemy of her but she did not know that.

Romantic Prompt # 33:

A girl fell in love with a poor, careless, & dirty boy. Why? What was good thing in this guy?

Romantic Prompt # 34:

She fell in love with a Robocop person who was empty of all emotions & feelings.

Romantic Prompt # 35:

A beautiful lady, who only trap to detective persons every time.

Romantic Prompt # 36:

Suddenly, she saw her husband who had disappeared 10 years ago.

Romantic Prompt # 37:

Your character is traveling by train, suddenly he saw a girl, who was continually staring him.

Romantic Prompt # 38:

She had been finding her lost husband for three years. Finally, she finds him a place, but he deny to recognize her.

Romantic Prompt # 39:

Your husband's mental condition is like that when she lie to him, husband consider a truth, but when she speak truth, husband think that she is lying.

Romantic Prompt # 40:

Her husband do opposite of her wife every time in everything.

Romantic Prompt # 41:

Your character sees a women's golden hair on your husband's shirt. She suspects him.

Romantic Prompt # 42:

Your character want to marry a girl, but in the engagement day, a secret is revealed on him, and he deny to marry her.

Romantic Prompt # 43:

Your character fell in love with a mental girl and he try to treatment.

Romantic Prompt # 44:

A criminal fell in love with a girl and he kidnap her.

Romantic Prompt # 45:

Your character comes to know that her daughter like a boy, so he investigate about that boy.

Romantic Prompt # 46:

He wanted to her daughter marriage with a boy, who like some else girl, but he was forced to marry. Why?

Romantic Prompt # 47:

Your character fell in love with a girl sitting in the passenger's bus. So he follows her.

Romantic Prompt # 48:

A girl cheats to your character, so your character trap her sister and cheat her as a revenge.

Romantic Prompt # 49:

He fell in love with her wife's friend.

Romantic Prompt # 50:

A teacher propose his student for marrying.

Romantic Prompt # 51:

Your character suspects that a girl is trying to trap him, but in fact, it was not true.

Romantic Prompt # 52:

A girl tells your character that her husband liked her before.

Romantic Prompt # 53:

He was going abroad to see his lover. He was seeing daydream. But when he reached there…

Romantic Prompt # 54:

He was trying to get that girl, but more he tried, the more she became far away.

Romantic Prompt # 55:

He married with his boss' girlfriend and boss get angry.

Romantic Prompt # 56:

Your character's lover said that she can't marry with him because she…

Romantic Prompt # 57:

A very unexpected visitor comes to your character's home… Your character never thought about that even in his dream.

Romantic Prompt # 58:

Your character likes a girl in Facebook, and then, she comes to your character's home.

Romantic Prompt # 59:

A girl comes to your character's shop and your character fell in love with her but doesn't express. One day she comes to your character's home.

Romantic Prompt # 60:

Your character receives a gift on thanks giving day and it is written on it…

Romantic Prompt # 61:

On charismas day, your character gifts a box to his lover. She got angry when she saw empty box. But in fact this box was not empty. She could not see the thing. What was that?

Romantic Prompt # 62:

Many peoples wanted to marry with a very beautiful girl, but she selected a very poor and old man for marriage. Why?

Romantic Prompt # 63:

Her fiancé when return his country, he had a wife with him.

Romantic Prompt # 64:

Someone tells your character that her fiancé is already married.

Romantic Prompt # 65:

After marriage, your character comes to know that his husband is a mental case.

Romantic Prompt # 66:

After marriage, your character comes to know that his husband had already divorced three wives before.

Romantic Prompt # 67:

Someone becomes to cause of separation between a couples.

Romantic Prompt # 68:

He married with her just for revenge but after that he fell in love with her.

Romantic Prompt # 69:

It was just a paper marriage and according to contract, he had to left her, but he fell in love with her.

Romantic Prompt # 70:

After five year of their love, he make a mistake and girl got angry and leave him.

Romantic Prompt # 71:

He had been trying to remove her anger for two years.

Romantic Prompt # 72:

Your character got a letter lying in the backyard and it is written "I love you, please meet me in this jungle at evening."

Romantic Prompt # 73:

One day, your character sees her wife talking with another boy in a restaurant.

Romantic Prompt # 74:

A virus comes in your computer and your important information hack.

Romantic Prompt # 75:

A girl says to your character that she fell in love with him in 2000 years ago.

Romantic Prompt # 76:

A person makes feel your character a more respectable person just for joy.

Romantic Prompt # 77:

A girl avenges of her sister and trap that guy, who cheated girl's sister.

Romantic Prompt # 78:

A person do a second marriage just for child and when he got child, he left his second wife.

Romantic Prompt # 79:

A beggar collects money and shift to another city and lives a luxury life.

Romantic Prompt # 80:

After fail in love, he start trying to get fame.

Romantic Prompt # 81:

A girl fell in love with him, but guy has a condition for marrying her and condition is that she would never born a child. Girl accepts his condition.

Romantic Prompt # 82:

A guy who wants to make his child a writer.

Romantic Prompt # 83:

A mother who says to her child to trap a girl. She wanted to take revenge of girl's father.

Romantic Prompt # 84:

One day, she opens his husband's cabinet and knows that her husband is a very big necromancer. He do black magic.

Romantic Prompt # 85:

A girl, who is trapping to her friend's husband.

Romantic Prompt # 86:

A husband, who suspects on her wife's loyalty without any reason.

Romantic Prompt # 87:

A writer, who make girls fall in love with him, just by writing romantic stories.

Romantic Prompt # 88:

Your character lost his way in stranger city.

Romantic Prompt # 89:

A person, who used to speaks truth, but because of his truth, he stuck in many problems.

Romantic Prompt # 90:

A person, who cast a spells for getting love of a girl, but girl start hating to him after his spells.

Romantic Prompt # 91:

A person buys an old mobile phone and in this mobile, there is a girl's picture. He fall in love with her.

Romantic Prompt # 92:

While going to the village, he saw a girl. He fall in love with her and try to get information about her, but all villagers don't know about her.

Romantic Prompt # 93:

Your character fall in love with a girl and hire his friend for information about her, but your friend trap her girl and girl fall involve with your character's friend.

Romantic Prompt # 94:

Your character goes to someone's party with his friend. Your character fall in love with a girl there, but the girl fall in love with your character's friend.

Romantic Prompt # 95:

Your character fall in love with a married girl. Your character wants divorce between them.

Romantic Prompt # 96:

He fall in love with a divorced girl, but girl don't trust his loyalty.

Romantic Prompt # 97:

A guy cheat her. After marriage of guy, girl decide to revenge.

Romantic Prompt # 98:

She can't see any couples happiness. So she become cause of every couple's separation.

Romantic Prompt # 99:

His friend is a big cheater. Both are very good friends. But the good guy always try to save girls with his friend's trappings.

Romantic Prompt # 100:

 He hires a girl to trap his business partner.

Romantic Prompt # 101:

She is detective and try to catch a criminal but fall in love with criminal.

Romantic Prompt # 102:

He said to his friend to trap his wife, so he could know that his wife is loyal with him or not.

Romantic Prompt # 103:

He never allows her wife to make up.

Romantic Prompt # 104:

He reject by a girl just because of his innocent. That girl don't like innocent peoples. Then, he changes himself into a genius person in one year. But now he trap & cheat her.

Romantic Prompt # 105:

He had been suspecting for 10 years on his wife's loyalty. His loyal wife sick of him and take divorce.

Romantic Prompt # 106:

He fall in love with a friend's fiancée.

Romantic Prompt # 107:

He receives a threat two times that if he would not give divorce to his wife, he would be killed.

Romantic Prompt # 108:

Everyone are looking to him with strange eyes. So he wonder why all peoples are looking him. Then he got it…

Romantic Prompt # 109:

She closed the door, and everyone became suspicious about her.

Romantic Prompt # 110:

She used to flirt with every girl. One day, he fell in love with a girl, but girl thought that he is flirting.

Romantic Prompt # 111:

He is waiting for a girl in a restaurant. Then, two angry guys comes to him.

Romantic Prompt # 112:

He is kidnapped and on gun point, he is forced to marry with a girl.

Romantic Prompt # 113:

He wants to divorce his wife. So he is finding some reason for divorce but fail. One day, he asks to his friend to trap his wife.

Romantic Prompt # 114:

His lover's mother don't allow them for marriage.

Romantic Prompt # 115:

Finally, they succeeded to agree with their parents for their marriage. But after that, guy deny to marriage in wedding's day. Why?

Romantic Prompt # 116:

A ghost comes between their loves.

Romantic Prompt # 117:

She hates her husband. So when husband comes to near her, she pretend like that some ghost is in her body.

Romantic Prompt # 118:

Your character hates her fiancée arranged by his parents. But after marriage, he fell in love with her.

Romantic Prompt # 119:

Your character online order a pizza, and a diamond necklace comes out form the pizza box.

Romantic Prompt # 120:

A girl, who take divorce from his husband in wedding's next day. Now she is doing that to his 8th husband. But husband deny to divorce her.

Romantic Prompt # 121:

A girls comes to your character and claim that she is wife of your character's husband.

Romantic Prompt # 122:

She sees her husband with a girl in a restaurant. She suspects him, and she doesn't know, that girl is a sister of her husband.

Romantic Prompt # 123:

He does two marriages, arrange marriage and love marriage. And his parents doesn't know about his love marriage.

Romantic Prompt # 124:

He never thought about it that his wife would cheat him. But he doesn't know that his wife is not cheating him, she is giving sacrifice for him.

Romantic Prompt # 125:

He was finding a girl, whom he saw on Facebook. After two years, he saw that girl in bazar.

Romantic Prompt # 126:

A poor boy fall in love with a richest girl. But girl think that boy is trapping her just because of getting wealth.

Romantic Prompt # 127:

A girl married with a boy without permission of his parents. After that, cheat her and goes out. The parent doesn't not know that she is married, so they decide to girl's marriage with a boy.

Romantic Prompt # 128:

They want to marry with each other. But girl's father doesn't like the boy and force to the boy for cheating with her.

Romantic Prompt # 129:

A father does marriage of his daughter with a boy, who cheated her daughter two years ago.

Romantic Prompt # 130:

A father does marriage of his daughter with a boy, whom daughter hates.

Romantic Prompt # 131:

She cheat an innocent boy, and after that, her boyfriend cheat her.

Romantic Prompt # 132:

Your character fall in love with a girl and has been sending gifts for one years. And girl doesn't know who is sending her gifts.

Romantic Prompt # 133:

Your shy character fell in love with his class fellow and doesn't express his feelings. One day, girl express her feeling of love with him.

Romantic Prompt # 134:

She fell in love with her boss, but boss cheat her. She traps boss's son for revenge.

Romantic Prompt # 135:

He receives a love letter of a girl by mistake, and he fell in love with her.

Romantic Prompt # 136:

She wants to do his husband's second marriage. Why?

Romantic Prompt # 137:

One day, your character comes to know that his loving & caring husband has another marriage too.

Romantic Prompt # 138:

Your character fell in love with a celebrity, he make a plan to get her.

Romantic Prompt # 139:

An enemy married with your character's fiancée. Your character take revenge, and trap enemy's sister.

Romantic Prompt # 140:

The daughter of your character's boss fall in love with him. The boss get angry and your character lost his job.

Romantic Prompt # 141:

They both loves to each other. They guy, who lives another country, died. Girl think that guy is cheating her. So girl travel to guy's country and found a person of guys' resemblance.

Romantic Prompt # 142:

They both loves to each other and no one express their feeling of love because of rejection.

Romantic Prompt # 143:

Your character' lover reject him because of his poverty. She likes only wealthy person. So your character start trying to became a wealthy person.

Romantic Prompt # 144:

A beggar's daughter traps to your character in her love.

Romantic Prompt # 145:

They loves to each other. When girl comes to know that her friend also love with her lover, she decide to sacrifice for her and leave his guy for her friend.

Romantic Prompt # 146:

Your character fell in love with a girl, whose father cheated your character' father in business.

Romantic Prompt # 147:

This is your character's love marriage. After marriage, your character comes to know that her father is a murderer of his father.

Romantic Prompt # 148:

Your character fell in love with a girl, who only like fashionable guys. So she reject him. Then, your character try hard to change himself and became a fashionable person in one year. After that, he become a very famous in girls and every girl want to marry her. Then, your character's lover start liking him and want to marry him. But now he is not interested in his lover and he rejects her.

Romantic Prompt # 149:

It is running treatment of half mental person. Soon, he feel better but now he fell in love with lady doctor. And situation becomes very complicated.

Romantic Prompt # 150:

Your character's boss is trying to find reason for fire him, but your character is so careful.

Romantic Prompt # 151:

In the restaurant, seeing a waitress, your character feel like that he knows her, but he is not remembering.

Romantic Prompt # 152:

Suddenly, she see a person, who cheated her, with her sister in restaurant.

Romantic Prompt # 153:

A 16-year-old boy fall in love with his teacher.

Romantic Prompt # 154:

While eating biscuit in the way, a girl threw an empty box of biscuit in dustbin. Then, a boy, who is following her, comes here and pick up the empty box.

Romantic Prompt # 155:

Two brothers fall in love with a girl.

Romantic Prompt # 156:

An old & wealthy man is finding a loyal boy for his daughter, but he knows that boys would marry her just because of his wealth. So he make a plan for finding a loyal boy for his daughter.

Romantic Prompt # 157:

Your character comes to know that her husband had murdered of his first wife.

Romantic Prompt # 158:

Suddenly, a person comes & say to your character in the restaurant "You have affair with my sister." And in fact, this is not true.

Romantic Prompt # 159:

Suddenly, a girl says to your character that they loved to each other 10 years ago and she had been finding him for 10 years.

Romantic Prompt # 160:

Your character's car hit a girl. She faint. Your character take her to the hospital and stuck in many problems.

Romantic Prompt # 161:

A thief fell in love with a girl. He leaves his profession of stealing & cobbering for getting her love.

Romantic Prompt # 162:

He had been finding his lover for many years. Finally, he finds him, but that is his bad luck. He finds her on girl's wedding day.

Romantic Prompt # 163:

She had been waiting for him for five years. And today, he is going to meet her.

Romantic Prompt # 164:

"You are right, I don't reserve for your love". He said sadly to her.

Romantic Prompt # 165:

This was a best time to ruin his life.

Romantic Prompt # 166:

It was not a marriage, it was sold her to someone.

Romantic Prompt # 167:

She is going to work on very foolish & horrible idea. She just wanted to see what would happen?

Romantic Prompt # 168:

Many people are looking to him, but your character don't care and he run towards her.

Romantic Prompt # 169:

He had not believe on first sight love, but one day…

Romantic Prompt # 170:

He was so important for her, but was unable to prove that.

Romantic Prompt # 171:

He has ability to freeze time, one day he sees a girl in the park and he freeze the time.

Romantic Prompt # 172:

A beautiful girl offer to your character to share her umbrella in rainy day

Romantic Prompt # 173:

"My one advice remember, if I could not return…" He started to say something to his lover.

Romantic Prompt # 174:

He found a beautiful girl's picture on the train.

Romantic Prompt # 175:

She pulled her knife and attack to him. In fact, she doesn't want to hurt him, but by mistake, she hurt him.

Romantic Prompt # 176:

After long time of her lonely life, she decided to make a boyfriend.

Romantic Prompt # 177:

She started to receive gift from unknown resources, but she had an idea who was sending her gifts.

Romantic Prompt # 178:

She comes to know a secret of her lover, and now she can't marry with him.

Romantic Prompt # 179:

They were competitor, but after that they fell in love with each other.

Romantic Prompt # 180:

After broking her heart, he fell in love with her.

Romantic Prompt # 181:

They are good friends and he fell in love with her but he doesn't want to take risk for going to next level.

Romantic Prompt # 182:

He was very unserious about his fake love, but she was very series.

Romantic Prompt # 183:

He is into in something but his lover doesn't like that.

Romantic Prompt # 184:

He promised to marry with her but because of some reason, he had to break his promise.

Romantic Prompt # 185:

He loves with a girl, but girl's many things cause to unhappy for him.

Romantic Prompt # 186:

He is trying to give good impression for first meeting. But it was worst.

Romantic Prompt # 187:

She love him, but he doesn't know that. He only knows her with reference of his cousin.

Romantic Prompt # 188:

He is very ugly looking, but she fell in love with him. And he just take her love non series.

Romantic Prompt # 189:

Your character does crazy thing to impress a girl.

Romantic Prompt # 190:

They loves each other, but a ghost start to visible to the girl. And boy doesn't believe on her.

Romantic Prompt # 191:

After death of her husband, parent wants her second marriage, but she doesn't want and flee away.

Romantic Prompt # 192:

She wants to marry with her cousin, but cousin treat her like his younger sister.

Romantic Prompt # 193:

For her treatment of mental mind, doctor suggest marriage. But who would be marry with a mental girl?

Romantic Prompt # 194:

He tried to trap a daughter of a business's man.

Romantic Prompt # 195:

For long times, she had been writing something. Her parents sees and shock.

Romantic Prompt # 196:

She was going to her husband in abroad. Their wedlock had happened in telephone 9 months ago.

Romantic Prompt # 197:

She doesn't want to go in her husband's family.

Romantic Prompt # 198:

She had been waiting for all day, and finally he comes but…

Romantic Prompt # 199:

Both sisters has same resemblance. So it is very hard for him to recognize his lover.

Romantic Prompt # 200:

"I can't live without you". She said to her husband who is going abroad.

Romantic Prompt # 201:

A very innocent person, who was very cruel in reality. Who could thought that? Only his wife knows that.

Romantic Prompt # 202:

She sees her last time, and return him engagement ring.

Romantic Prompt # 203:

She had been talking with her lover for long time. Now it had midnight. She depart from there for her home and …

Romantic Prompt # 204:

She keeps an impossible condition for marrying.

Romantic Prompt # 205:

He don't like his sister's lover. So he made a plan.

Romantic Prompt # 206:

In the book store, a girl is finding a same book that guy is finding. From here their love story starts.

Romantic Prompt # 207:

She throws a water on her friend, but by mistake, water fell on a guy. Start a love story from here.

Romantic Prompt # 208:

She fell in love with online teacher that live on another city.

Romantic Prompt # 209:

He is taxi driver, he pick & drop a passenger who is a beautiful girl. Girl fell in love with taxi driver, and she left her visiting card intentionally on car.

Romantic Prompt # 210:

In a shopping mall, he fell in love with an 18 years old girl.

Chapter 7:

SCI-FIC, ACTION & ADVENTURES WRITING PROMPTS

Adventures Prompt # 01:

Your fiction character is driving a car in the deep jungle. Suddenly, he saw a big horrible creature standing in the road. The creature is about to attacked to his car. What happened next? What should your character do now?

Adventures Prompt # 02:

Your fiction hero character is traveling by air. Suddenly, aero plane become out of control and pilot say that aero plane is about to fell in upcoming moments. All passenger are scared. But your character do something strange for saving all lives.

Adventures Prompt # 03:

Your character is running at lonely place, some creature is following him. He sees a building and he enter into the building. He astonish when he sees another horrible creature in the building.

Adventures Prompt # 04:

Since past one months, there have been some beast living in the jungle. And they daily catch and eat one human being from near the city. City's people are becoming very worried. So Government call to the expert team for killing the beasts. Your fiction hero character is the part of this team.

Adventures Prompt # 05:

Whoever goes to this jungle, never comes back. Many teams went for investigation but could not come back.

Adventures Prompt # 06:

Treasure in the cave...whoever went to this cave for get this, died. Your character goes there with his friends.

Adventures Prompt # 07:

Your character working on water pipe line. Suddenly, he slipped and get into the pipe line and faint. After waking up, he find himself in old century.

Adventures Prompt # 08:

A strange being is chasing to your character for killing.

Adventures Prompt # 09:

Many strange beings started coming in the city. Who are these?

Adventures Prompt # 10:

His boat lost its way and a big crocodile is following your character's boat.

Adventures Prompt # 11:

Some aliens want to occupy to all world.

Adventures Prompt # 12:

A scientists invests such a thing, who would wear this thing, would become an invisible man.

Adventures Prompt # 13:

Aliens comes on the city, and start kidnaping of the peoples.

Adventures Prompt # 14:

A scientist invent such a thing, and now everyone can reach to anyplace by telephone call.

Adventures Prompt # 15:

Some scientist criminals invent such a thing for controlling to the sun.

Adventures Prompt # 16:

His was a half human and was a half lion.

Adventures Prompt # 17:

Their boat lost their way and they reach an island, where they find a lots of idols.

Adventures Prompt # 18:

Two friend was travelling just for fun and they reach at 1-inch-little-man's world.

Adventures Prompt # 19:

They goes to mountain and then, a big foot sees them and reach to the city by following them, and then, big foot create problems in the city.

Adventures Prompt # 20:

An aero plane is about fall on your character's house.

Adventures Prompt # 21:

Your character reaches in his past via black hole, and correct his mistake and live a new life.

Adventures Prompt # 22:

There is a big reassure in an old well. Many peoples tried to get this one, but…

Adventures Prompt # 23:

A big spider is killing to human of your character's city.

Adventures Prompt # 24:

Your character reaches an island, where human being is opposite, their heads are on down and legs are up.

Adventures Prompt # 25:

Two friend goes to the jungle, and forget their way of return.

Adventures Prompt # 26:

Some friends goes to a valley for picnic and face a strange problem.

Adventures Prompt # 27:

Some friends goes to somewhere and their two friends disappear.

Adventures Prompt # 28:

Their car stop in the jungle and there are many wolves howling around their car.

Adventures Prompt # 29:

A scientist, who fail after reaching at 99% of his success. But then, an ordinary person solve the problem.

Adventures Prompt # 30:

Suddenly, all dogs of the city start drinking human blood. So they are attacking.

Adventures Prompt # 31:

Your character goes to the jungle with his friends for picnic. There, they got a cabin and in the cabin, there are skulls and bones of human beings.

Adventures Prompt # 32:

Your character have to go abroad for catching strange criminal.

Adventures Prompt # 33:

A kangaroo kidnap children from the city. Your character try to catch him.

Adventures Prompt # 34:

Your character got a map of treasure that is in the north side jungle.

Adventures Prompt # 35:

An animal is created because of a scientist's mistake, and animal start killing to the humans in the city.

Adventures Prompt # 36:

Because of a chemical reaction, a doctor become an animal.

Adventures Prompt # 37:

A strange animal comes in the city and kills to the human beings. Your character is hunter, so he try to catch him.

Adventures Prompt # 38:

Your character discovers that there are some strange beings are living the other side of mountain.

Adventures Prompt # 39:

Some aliens are standing in his home's backyard.

Adventures Prompt # 40:

A motor boat, that was going to abroad, disappeared. Your character's mission is to find that boat.

Adventures Prompt # 41:

Five friends are going to a mountain. When they reach at top of the mountain, they left two, remaining three friends had dead.

Adventures Prompt # 42:

Write something on Friendship of goat & elephant.

Adventures Prompt # 43:

A lion, who catch a child daily. All villagers are worried. Then, a young boy take stand for it.

Adventures Prompt # 44:

A very weak & skinny boy catch and kill a tiger with his weak hand.

Adventures Prompt # 45:

A house of village is burning and dead bodies are being got out.

Adventures Prompt # 46:

He had been creating a strange dress for long time. Finally, he got success. Now his behavior changed after wearing this strange dress. That was what he want.

Adventures Prompt # 47:

He was trying to kills a lion, but lion disappeared.

Adventures Prompt # 48:

He had to go to the jungle for finding his lost friends.

Adventures Prompt # 49:

Suddenly, his friend got mad and tried to kill their all friends after seeing treasure in the jungle.

Adventures Prompt # 50:

A wolf, who comes in the city on only 14th date of moon and then, take a child. Your character make plan to catch him.

Chapter 8:

PROMPTS – THREE ELEMETNS

Write a story that contains all these three elements or items.

1. A flower, Detective and murder of a scientist
2. A stolen cell phone, a Young man and a big party
3. Nightmare, a mysterious tree and a young girl
4. A friend's house, a weird thing, and Friend's angry father
5. The ghost, a lamp and money
6. A Happy Wife, a park and a little poor child
7. A party, an old enemy and a poison cake
8. A cave, a lion, and a woodcutter
9. A true dream, lover and a shocking news
10. An email, fear of death, Young lady
11. Necromancer, jungle, car
12. Beautiful waitress, stranger, proposal
13. Mountain, prince, fairy,
14. Broken keyboard, old store, trouble maker
15. Jungle, hut, mysterious man
16. Lipstick, two thieves, bicycle
17. Home's door, dead body of hen, necromancer
18. Tree, dead Boyd, ring
19. Fear of die, gift, dream meaning teller
20. Passenger's bus, empty pistol, old lady
21. Carve, diamond ring, snake
22. Message on the phone, dead body, empty & lonely old form house
23. Blue eyes, dream, misunderstanding
24. Ocean, ring, strange being,
25. Hotel's room, secret, death
26. Watch, spy camera, gift
27. Girl, love, revenge,
28. New friend, revenge, murder

29. Cabinet, knife, murderer,
30. Golden hair, dead body, message,
31. Suicide, shoes, blood
32. Car, brake fail, trap
33. Valentine day, gift, fear
34. Shop, beautiful girl, kidnap
35. Pain in the teeth, faint, mysterious room
36. Return of stealing mobile phone, threat, murder
37. Storm, tree, map of treasure,
38. Island, debris of motor boat, a lot of human skulls,
39. Mail, perfume, murder
40. Smuggling, murderer, coffin,
41. Owl's blood, black magic, backyard,
42. Second floor, lift, stranger
43. Faint person, road, car
44. Girl, car, pistol
45. Poison food, cat, guest,
46. Hotel, dead body, criminal,
47. Accident, love, stranger girl,
48. Rope, girl, car
49. Traveler, valley, old man
50. Poison flower, letter, enemy
51. Facebook, friendship, trap,
52. Rainy day, stranger, stealing
53. Wolf, child, stranger
54. Murder of beggar, secret, private detective
55. TV, drops of blood, afraid security guard,
56. New neighbor, scream, ghost
57. Fear of digit 7, secret, stranger
58. Broken bottle of drink, one shoe, marks of blood,
59. Old car, jungle, golden ring
60. Diamond, mountain, trap
61. School, love, student
62. Child, shoes, car
63. Hotel, waiter, poison
64. Rich girl, poor boy, true love
65. Train master, ghost, dead body

66. Broken mobile phone, call, faint
67. Train, robber, jungle
68. Picnic party, mountain, big foot,
69. Smell, dead body on the roof, message
70. Driver, passenger, ghost
71. Mysterious building, ball, joke
72. Beautiful snake, road, friendship
73. Coffin, stealing, diamond
74. Cemetery, criminal, plan
75. Robber, faint, car
76. Taxi, amount, passenger
77. Fisherman, pound, golden bracelet,
78. Tree, dead body, sign of eagle
79. Island, criminal, children,
80. Boat, blood, rope
81. Message, car, brake fail,
82. Hunter, horrible lion, rope
83. Empty house, criminal, ghost
84. Empty house, nail cutter, rope
85. Hotel, 4 children, secret
86. Box of glass, child, alien
87. Map, wooden box, cave
88. Camera, idol, room
89. Digging, doll, two diamond
90. Well, box, old jewelry,
91. Jungle, tree, voices
92. Tree, little boy, vanished
93. Strange person, city, fear
94. Packet, cat, servant,
95. Dance, shoe, faint,
96. Accident, murderer, criminal
97. Locked closet, diary, criminal,
98. Diary, one thousand age, ghost
99. School, bag, mysterious thing
100. Alien, message, death
101. Petrol pump, dangerous, mobile phone
102. House on rent, blood, sound

103. Car, knife, enemy
104. Party, murderer, trap
105. Stranger, bouquet, old love
106. Child, kidnap, security guard
107. Apple, knife, murderer
108. Mysteries jungle, dead car, fear
109. Fisherman, ocean, secret
110. Stranger, misunderstand, love
111. Axe, blood, innocent
112. Snake, trap, house
113. Two faces, hate, love
114. Innocent person, girl, changing
115. Stealing of snake, criminal, murder
116. One night, mistake, love
117. Head quarter, flee of criminal, trap
118. Girl, love, murder
119. Hotel, criminal, resembling
120. Kitchen, dead body, reel in the window
121. Flower of the autumn, fear, government,
122. Husband, sincerity, money
123. Cave, kidnapped children, snake
124. Alien, love, trap
125. Dead body, needle, close window
126. Terrorist, secret, hawker
127. Stolen car, ring, faint person
128. Necromancer, faint person, stealing
129. Murder of criminal, message, travel
130. Lost island, travel, mysterious light
131. Bear, bone, secret
132. Message written on sky, criminal, murder
133. Wealth, trap, strange email
134. City, mysterious person, fear
135. Fear of goat, neighborhood, ghost
136. Empty castle, spirit, car
137. Comb, death, trap
138. Cycle, fear, faint
139. Job, death of boss, investigation

140. Road, digging, dead body
141. Broken wall, skull, knife
142. Bathroom, scream, piece of human hand
143. Stolen diary, secret, problem
144. Mysterious diary, fear, murder
145. Criminal, car, idol
146. College, examination, stealing
147. Broken umbrella, lost person, jungle,
148. Smuggling, fisherman's village, detective
149. Court, innocent person, criminal
150. Jungle, car, to disappear a bag
151. Room, smell, digging,
152. Scientist, to lost memory, trap
153. Scientist formula, cave, to lost
154. Tree, stealing, investigation
155. Criminal, spy camera, hotel
156. Mysterious castle, criminal, ghost
157. Stolen ring, fear of death, message
158. Daughter, love, cheater boy
159. Enemy, silly human, clever friend
160. Amount, bus, trick
161. Witness, criminal, ghost
162. Spirit, revenge, murder
163. Property, innocent person, revenge
164. Wedding night, to flee with terror, divorce
165. Robbers, kidnap, ghost
166. Chair, invisible entity, voice
167. Chair, rope, knife
168. Car, cylinder, drugs
169. Box of sweets, gift, strange thing
170. Travel, lover, disappointing
171. First meeting, lover, strange movements
172. Biscuit, dead body, clue
173. Travelling, watch, bomb
174. Phone booth, stolen ring, pocket
175. Aero plane, fault in engine, trapping
176. Taxi, passenger's bag, forgetting

177. Car, stranger, knife
178. Roof, blood, ax
179. Investigation, ghost, criminal
180. Assistant running, message, detective surprising
181. A wish, trying, success
182. Resemblance, lost brother, bazar
183. Detective, scream for help, criminal
184. Doctor, scream, trapping
185. Doctor, kidnapping, boss's sickness
186. Curtain, ghost, shadow,
187. Empty room, noises, ghost
188. Guest, love, unexpected thing
189. Music concert, invitation card, amazing thing,
190. Valentine day, revenge, mysterious message
191. Close room, crying, midnight
192. Cold night, hailing, terrifying thing
193. lamps' light, old man, fear
194. jungle, hut, pieces of human hand
195. old room, lock, ghost
196. snake, bushes, 10 years boy
197. mobile phone, secret, enemy
198. train, big foot, cannel,
199. night, trying to suicide, ghost
200. little boy on the door, night, problems
201. poor man, mysterious faintness, changing
202. five friend, adventure, murder
203. three friend, picnic, problems on return
204. enemy, good behaviors, to surprise
205. hut in the jungle, wolf, dangers
206. empty room, talking, fear
207. phone call, stranger, beautiful voice
208. wrong phone call, beautiful voice, action,
209. raining, stolen ring, stranger
210. singer, stealing, investigation
211. fear, diamond, black person wearing black clothes
212. bus, stolen ring, problem
213. guest, trapping, black magic

214. handkerchief, perfume, criminal,
215. jungle, well, prince
216. bridal, ghost, old house
217. crocodile, fisherman, storm in river
218. lizard, horrible house, necklace,
219. bread, meat, horrible human being
220. tea, cigar, blood
221. snake, luxury house, secret,
222. ghee, lizard, dead body
223. computer, voice, ghost
224. jacket, bottle, spider
225. shifting, happiness, frightened after two days
226. washing machine, secret, ghost
227. wolf, child, kidnap
228. diary, jungle, lonely & strange human being
229. rainy day, ghost, shelter
230. umbrella, blood, clues of criminal

Chapter 7:

NARRATIVE PROMPTS

Narrative Prompt # 01

Write an unforgettable event of your life, that you could not forget until now.

Narrative Prompt # 02

It is your first day of your job. And you are preparing for go to your office. Write a scene of 500 words.

Narrative Prompt # 03

In your school days, how did you spend your holiday?

Narrative Prompt # 04

In childhood, who was your ideal personality? Is that any teacher, singer, actor or someone else?

Narrative Prompt # 05

Did you travel on public transport? Write some memorable happening in the public transport that you could not forget.

Narrative Prompt # 06

In your childhood, when you wanted to eat something or buy something, then how did you say to your parents for this?

Narrative Prompt # 07

Imagine, you are receiving some grand reward, so how would you feel. Write a feeling about your excitements and happiness.

Narrative Prompt # 08

Imagine, you fell in love with a girl, who is student of your college or university, then, how would you tell her about your feeling? Or you would not tell her.

Narrative Prompt # 09

Write about some prank that you did with some person or friend.

Narrative Prompt # 10

If your favorite fiction book character come to see you suddenly, how would you react?

Narrative Prompt # 11

Write about a time, when you became really surprised in your life.

Narrative Prompt # 12

When did you really feel happiness when someone gave you a gift? Gift that made you a full of happiness.

Narrative Prompt # 13

When do you get really angry or annoyed, when someone say or do…? What?

Narrative Prompt # 14

Write about your first day in your college life.

Narrative Prompt # 15

If it is going to fill full your one desire, and you have to choose one option, which one will you choose? (1) A lot of money (2) your love (3) go to past & correct your mistake

Narrative Prompt # 16

Do you believe on arrange marriage or love marriage & tell us why?

Narrative Prompt # 17

You love one girl/boy, and he/she love another one. Also one girl/boy loves you, then you have an option to choose for marriage, which one do you prefer for marrying?

Narrative Prompt # 18

If you are not a human being, what can you be? What thought come in your mind first?

Narrative Prompt # 19

If you have an option to correct your past mistake. Which mistake you would like to correct? Which mistake give you regret?

Narrative Prompt # 20

What is your profession right now? It you don't have that profession, then what else profession you have? For example, if you are computer operator, and if you are not be a computer operator, you could be a writer.

Narrative Prompt # 21

If you comes to know that your parents is not your real parents and your real parents are those who live in another city. How do you react?

Narrative Prompt # 22

If you propose some girl and then she told you that she don't like you. What would you do?

Narrative Prompt # 23

You have been struggling for achieving your goal/career. Now you have a chance to achieve this. But if you do that your love would be lose. So which one option would you choose, your love or your career and why?

Narrative Prompt # 24

What do you do when you get really tired, but you have to finish your work?

Narrative Prompt # 25

Which thing scared you most?

Narrative Prompt # 26

When do you feel more nervous? And you can't control yourself in spite of your struggling?

Narrative Prompt # 27

If you have a chance to take revenge with your enemy. What punishment would you choose?

Narrative Prompt # 28

What things make you really sad?

Narrative Prompt # 29

Write about an experienced, when you learnt something newly like car driving or something else.

Narrative Prompt # 30

Which thing is more important for you, and you never compromise on this.

Narrative Prompt # 31

Do you believe in ghost?

Narrative Prompt # 32

Write a situation, whenever you though to something a ghost.

Narrative Prompt # 33

If a ghost comes in front of you, how do you react?

Narrative Prompt # 34

If you got a dead body in your car, how would you react?

Narrative Prompt # 35

Write about your mistake, that you feel regret.

Narrative Prompt # 36

Write three good things and three bad things or habit about you.

Narrative Prompt # 37

Which quality in you feel you proud?

Narrative Prompt # 38

Do you have any lack that makes you feel inferiority complex?

Narrative Prompt # 39

Write some such a funny moment in your life that you can't forget.

Narrative Prompt # 40:

If you have a chance to reach in your past, then, how would be your life?

THE END